Author:

Fiona Macdonald studied history at Cambridge University and at the university of East Anglia. She has taught children, adults and undergraduates. She has written many books on historical topics, mainly for children.

Illustrator:

John James was born in London in 1959. He studied at Eastbourne College of Art and has specialised in historical reconstruction since leaving art school in 1982.

Series creator:

David Salariya is an illustrator, designer and author. He is the founder of the Salariya Book Company, which specialises in the creation and publication of books for young people, from babies to teenagers, under its imprints Book House and Scribblers.

Consultant:

John Gillingham studied history at Oxford and Munich universities. Since 1966 he has taught history at the London School of Economics and Political Science. He is the author of books on Richard the Lionheart, the Angevin Empire and the Wars of the Roses. He has also written and presented a TV programme on the Magna Carta.

Editor: Design assistant:
Vicki Power   **Carol Attwood**

© The Salariya Book Company Ltd MMIX

First published in hardback in Great Britain
in MCMXCI by
Book House, an imprint of
The Salariya Book Company Ltd
25 Marlborough Place, Brighton BN1 1UB

SALARIYA

Visit our website at **www.book-house.co.uk**
or go to **www.salariya.com**
for **free** electronic versions of:
You Wouldn't Want to be an Egyptian Mummy!
You Wouldn't Want to be a Roman Gladiator!
Avoid Joining Shackleton's Polar Expedition!
Avoid Sailing on a 19th-Century Whaling Ship!

ISBN 978-1-906714-88-8

A CIP catalogue record for this book is available
from the British Library.

Printed and bound in China.

CONTENTS

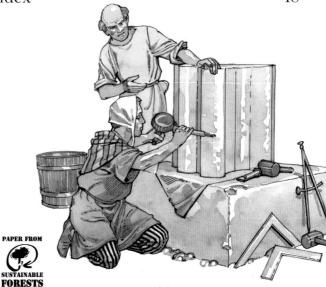

Medieval Cathedral

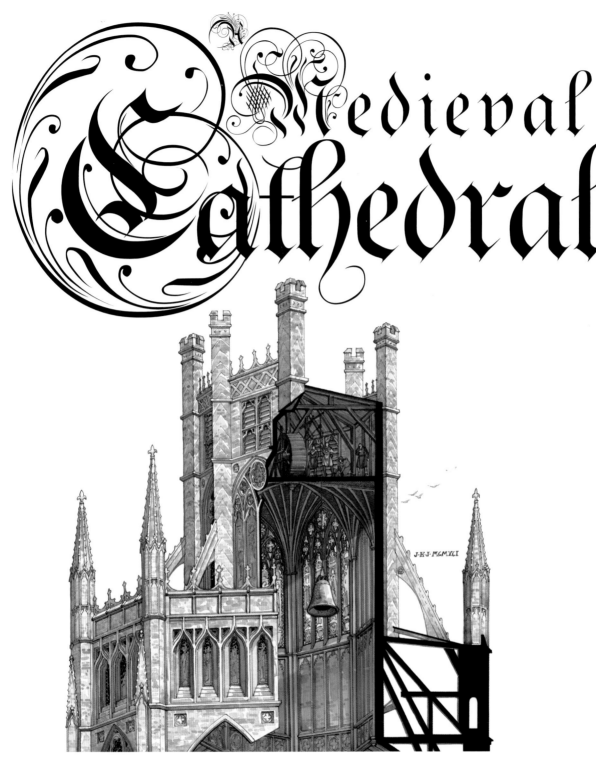

Written by
Fiona Macdonald

Series created by
David Salariya

Illustrated by
John James

BOOK HOUSE

INTRODUCTION

Throughout Europe, we can still see many beautiful medieval cathedrals towering above the rooftops of all but the tallest modern office blocks. These 'prayers in stone' have survived for centuries, and can still astonish us with their size and grandeur. Today, we admire their beauty, and marvel at the skills of the masons and carpenters who built them. We study them for what they have to tell us about the past, and worry about how to preserve them from decay and pollution. And we respect them as holy places, where people offer prayers and praises to God. The cathedrals shown in this book were mostly built during the Middle Ages (from around 550 to 1450). This was the great age of cathedral-building in Europe. Of course, building did not stop at the end of the medieval period: magnificent new cathedrals are still being constructed today. Now, as then, cathedrals display the might and majesty of the Church; like them, its power and glory seemed certain to endure forever.

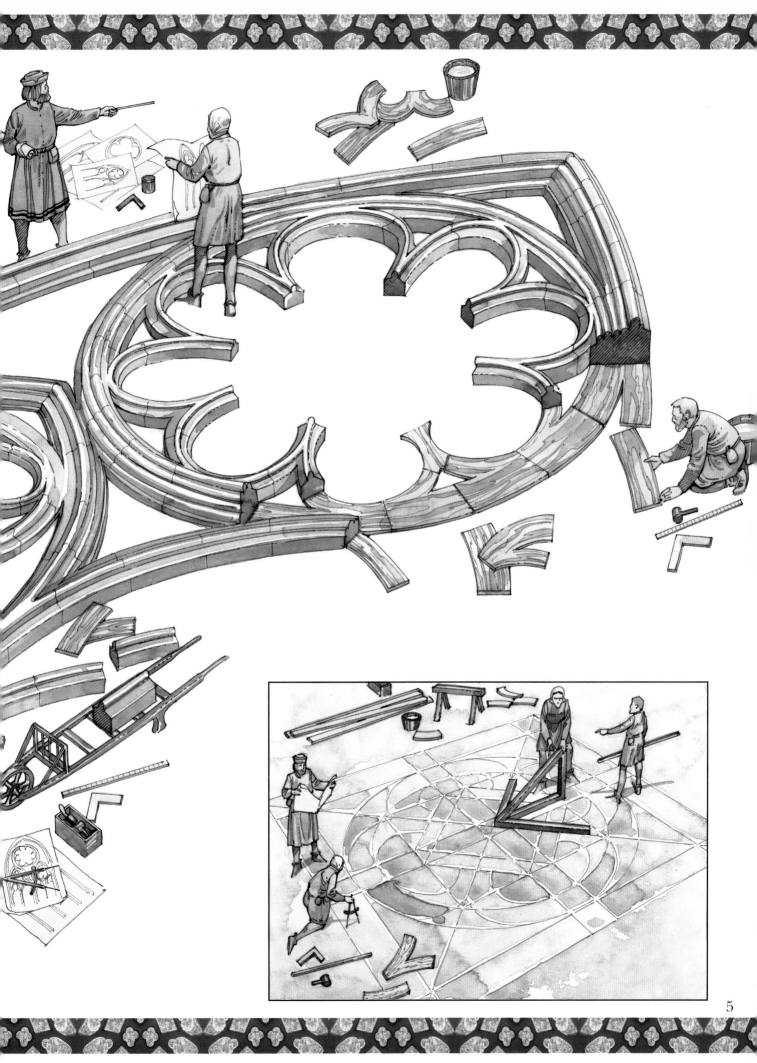

Choosing the site

In the Middle Ages, as today, the Christian world was divided into regions (called 'sees' or 'dioceses') for the purposes of Church government and administration. Each diocese was ruled by a bishop – a senior clergyman. Medieval bishops usually came from noble or wealthy families. Many of them were well educated, capable and energetic, and some played a leading part in running the countries in which their dioceses were situated. Not all bishops were conscientious about performing their religious duties. Some used their authority to help them fulfil personal ambitions for wealth and power.

A cathedral is the place where a bishop has his headquarters. The Church's power is symbolised by the bishop's throne (*cathedra* in Greek), a magnificent raised seat in the holiest part of the cathedral where the bishop sits during services. Medieval bishops chose to build their cathedrals in important towns or cities in their dioceses. Often, a cathedral was built on the site of an earlier church, particularly if it contained holy relics or had been founded by a saint.

The money to build cathedrals came mostly from gifts – of land, farms, houses and jewels, and gold and silver coins. People believed that by giving to the Church, they would help to win forgiveness for their sins.

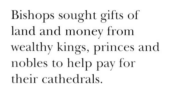

Bishops sought gifts of land and money from wealthy kings, princes and nobles to help pay for their cathedrals.

Cathedrals were very expensive to build and maintain. They needed frequent repairs, especially to the roof.

Many cathedrals were built on the site of earlier, smaller churches. Over the years, bishops added splendid new buildings to their cathedrals to house the clergy who worshipped there. Sometimes houses and shops had to be pulled down to make room; this could lead to trouble between the bishop and the townspeople.

Stages in the development of cathedrals: Roman hall, 2nd century AD.

Early oratory (place of prayer), built of wood with simple doorway and window, 627.

Stone-built church with round-arched doors and windows, from the 7th century.

Porch

Larger stone church with rounded apse and porch to protect door, Viking period, c. 780.

Apse

Bishop's throne, or *cathedra*, built in Canterbury Cathedral, England, around 1200, to replace an older one.

Workmen clear the site for a new cathedral.

J·F·J· MCMXCI

CATHEDRAL ARCHITECTURE

Cathedrals were founded throughout Europe in the Middle Ages, and, in later centuries, have been built all over the world following the spread of the Christian religion. All cathedrals, wherever they are, have the same religious function, which has not changed over the years. As one 5th-century writer put it: 'Let there be a throne towards the east, and places for priests to the right and left…the altar ought also to be there…'

Key elements – the bishop's throne, places for clergy (later known as the 'choir') and an altar, where the bishops and priests could celebrate Mass – were found in all cathedrals. In time, extra elements – a nave, where ordinary people stood, chapels to house the relics of saints or an altar dedicated to the Virgin Mary, and towers and spires where bells were hung – were added to cathedrals to meet the needs of the priests and people who worshipped there. Monasteries were attached to many European cathedrals, and the bishop's palace was built nearby.

Medieval cathedrals were built in a wide variety of architectural styles, according to the inventiveness of the cathedral's architect, the fashion of the time, and the tastes of the people who paid for them. This book contains many different examples of cathedral architecture.

Key

1. Aisle A sideways extension of the nave. ('Aisle' comes from the old French word for 'wing'.)

2. Arcade A row of arches supported by columns or pillars.

3. Buttress A prop of stone to stop the walls collapsing outwards under the weight of the roof.

4. Bell tower A tower where bells were hung, almost always at the west end of the cathedral. Bells were rung to call worshippers to services.

5. Clerestory A row of windows high up, designed to let extra light into the church or cathedral.

6. Choir The most holy end of the cathedral, nearest the altar. Cathedral clergy stood in the choir during services.

7. Flying Buttress A narrow, graceful buttress shaped like half an arch.

8. Foundation A strong platform several metres below ground.

9. Nave The 'body' of the cathedral, where worshippers stood or knelt during services.

10. Porch Provided shelter for worshippers and clergy.

11. Roof Covered with lead or sometimes slates or tiles, resting on a framework of wooden rafters.

12. Rose window A large, circular window filled with brilliantly patterned glass. Rose windows symbolised eternity.

13. Spire A tall, pointed structure built on top of one or more towers. Spires were built of wood, and covered with sheets of lead or with wooden tiles, known as shingles. Spires were often topped with a golden weather vane or a cross.

14. Transept A crosswise extension to the cathedral, usually located where the nave joins the choir. Transepts housed robing rooms for clergy and chapels dedicated to saints.

15. Vault The arched underside of the roof; the area that worshippers inside the building saw when they looked upwards.

QUARRYING THE STONE

The earliest Christian churches had been built of wood, or whatever was the cheapest and most readily available building material locally. But gradually, the Church grew more powerful and wealthy. More and more people began to follow its teachings – or as many of them as they felt able to follow. Bishops and priests began to build new and more magnificent churches and cathedrals. To do this, they chose the finest, most long-lasting materials available. Whenever possible, they chose to build their new cathedrals in stone.

Stone was hacked from the face of the quarry by hand, and hauled laboriously to the surface, using cranes or pulleys powered by men and animals. Quarrying was an exhausting, dangerous job. Quarry workers fell ill with diseases caused by dust and damp, and were often horribly injured in rock-falls and landslips. Despite the dangers of the job, they were very poorly paid.

Masons' tools (left to right): picks and axes for quarrying and shaping stone; hammer and chisel for dressing stone; saw for cutting stone; masons' bucket with lugs (handles) for lifting.

Rock face

Pick

The best building stone in Europe came from France. It was very expensive, largely because of the cost of transport from the quarry to the building site. In 1287, the builders of Norwich Cathedral in England ordered a load of stone from Caen, about 480 km away in northern France. The stone itself cost £1. 6s. 8d. (£1.33p), but loading and transport cost £3. 2s. 0d. (£3.10p) – almost twice as much again.

Many quarries had a blacksmith's forge (below, left) and workshop on site, to make, mend and sharpen the iron tools used to cut the stone.

Masons worked in lodges (simple huts) which provided shelter from rain, wind and sun, and also served as a place for relaxing and meeting with co-workers.

Shed for dressing (shaping) the stone

Masons' lodge

Blacksmith's forge

Winch

Sawing

Star chisel

Feather

Carver's chisel

Square

J·E·J· MCMXCI

Quarries were dangerous places. Workmen climbed down to the workface by means of wooden scaffolding and ladders. Floods and landslips often caused accidents.

Above: Cutting the stone. First, blocks were roughly sawn into shape – hard and exhausting work. Then the mason made a row of holes in the surface of the block, using a star-chisel and a mallet (a heavy hammer).

A metal tool called a 'feather' was then hammered into the stone, along the row of holes. This split the stone neatly and precisely. Finally, the stone was shaped by the carver with a fine chisel and a lighter mallet.

FOUNDATIONS

The second most important building material used in medieval cathedrals was wood. Oak was the best timber – it was beautiful to look at, hard, strong, and lasted for centuries. Like good-quality stone, it was expensive to buy, and even more expensive to transport.

Whenever possible it was carried by water, since this was the easiest and cheapest method of moving heavy loads in medieval times. Otherwise, wood was loaded onto carts pulled by horses or oxen, and hauled along bumpy roads to the nearest port.

Lighter, less durable wood such as pine or ash was used to make the scaffolding, ladders and all kinds of lifting machinery used in building the great cathedrals. And, of course, the ships and carts used to carry the stone and timber were themselves made out of wood.

While the wood and stone were being chosen and transported, workers at the building site were busy laying out the foundations. It might take hundreds of years to complete a cathedral, but the overall shape was often planned right from the start.

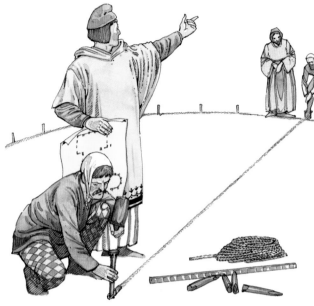

Marking out the foundations for a new cathedral building with ropes and wooden pegs, to provide a guide for the workmen digging the foundation trenches.

Medieval surveyors did not have modern instruments to help them. To make straight lines and square corners, they measured using a right-angled triangle.

Limestone was the most popular medieval building stone because it was easy to work.

Right: plan of a typical cathedral, showing walls and windows, and also the positions of the pillars supporting the roof. There is a large porch, known as a 'galilee', at the west end, and a semicircular space, known as an 'apse', at the east end. The nave was where ordinary people stood or knelt to hear services, while the cathedral clergy stood in the choir. There were extra chapels (places for prayer) in the transepts, and a central tower was built above the space where the nave joined the choir. Deep foundations had to be dug beneath the building to help support the huge weight of the cathedral.

Thousands of trees were needed to build a cathedral. Oak was the best and strongest wood, but by the 12th century it was already becoming scarce and expensive, and in France people complained about the great oak forests being cut down for building.

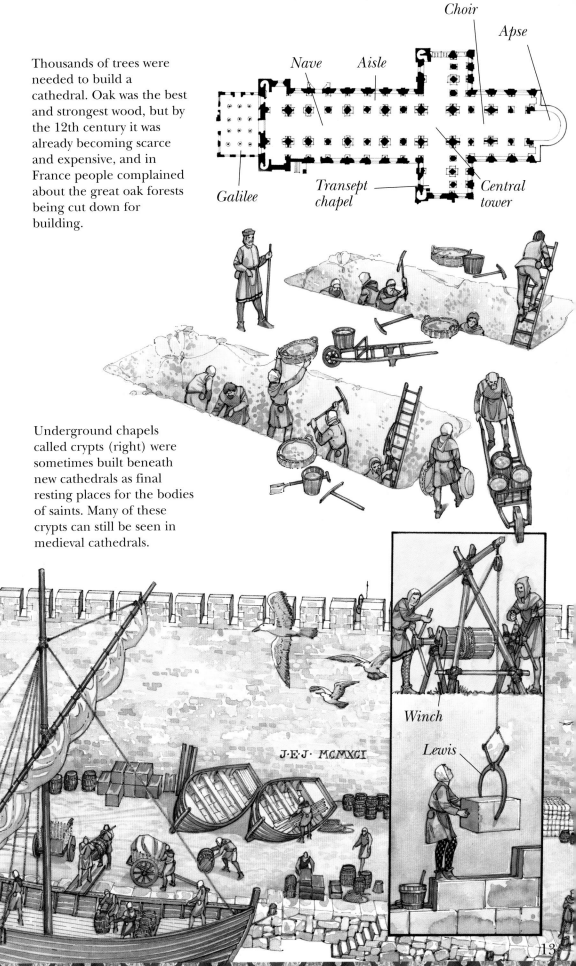

Choir

Apse

Nave *Aisle*

Galilee

Transept chapel

Central tower

Underground chapels called crypts (right) were sometimes built beneath new cathedrals as final resting places for the bodies of saints. Many of these crypts can still be seen in medieval cathedrals.

J·E·J· MCMXCI

Winch

Lewis

CRAFTSMEN

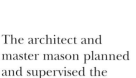

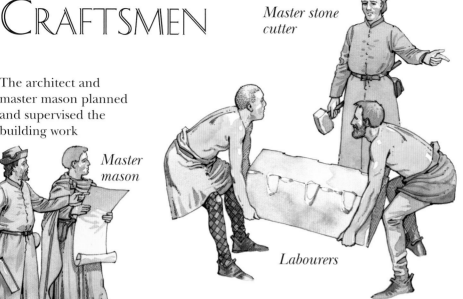

Master stone cutter

Stone dresser

The architect and master mason planned and supervised the building work

Master mason

Architect

Labourers carried the stones from wagons and barges to the site.

Labourers

The master cutter chose the best blocks of stone for each purpose.

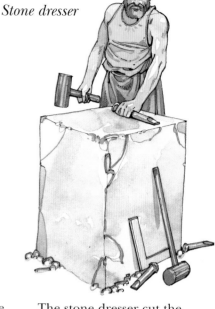

The stone dresser cut the stone into rough shape for the sculptors.

Medieval cathedrals, constructed hundreds of years ago, are still among the largest buildings in the world. With a few exceptions, their walls, towers and foundations have remained strong for centuries, and the beauty and magnificence of their structures – as well as the inventiveness of their design – still have the power to astonish and delight.

The men responsible for planning the layout and construction of the cathedrals were known as architect-engineers. (In the Middle Ages, there was no opportunity for women to study architecture, or to work on building sites.) They were highly skilled and, once they had made a name for themselves, they were in great demand all over Europe.

Carpenters made strong scaffolding to support windows and arches while they were being built.

Most cathedral roofs were wooden, with massive oak timbers for the beams and rafters.

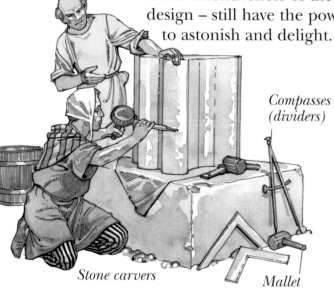

Compasses (dividers)

Stone carvers

Mallet

The stone carvers shaped stone into graceful and elaborate patterns for use in window frames, doorways and arches.

Carpenters

Plane

Bow saw

Auger

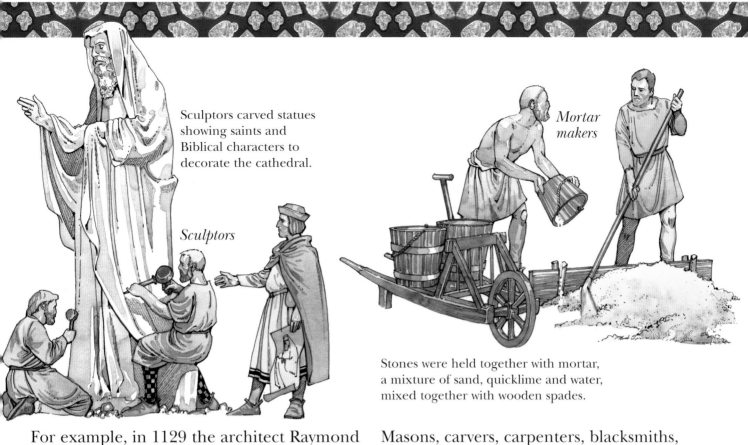

Sculptors carved statues showing saints and Biblical characters to decorate the cathedral.

Sculptors

Mortar makers

Stones were held together with mortar, a mixture of sand, quicklime and water, mixed together with wooden spades.

For example, in 1129 the architect Raymond agreed his fees with the archbishop. Each year he was to be paid six silver coins, 36 lengths of cloth, 17 loads of wood, as many shoes and gaiters as he required, plus two shillings per month, with a measure of salt and a pound of wax for candles – an expensive luxury.

Masons, carvers, carpenters, blacksmiths, roofers and glaziers were also paid well for their work. In early 14th-century England, master masons earned about 20 pence a week, about double what a farm worker might get. They were helped on site by labourers and rough workmen, and by apprentices practising their skills.

Blacksmiths repaired and sharpened building tools and also made decorative ironwork.

Roofer

Anvil

Blacksmith

Plumbers (lead workers) coated cathedral roofs with sheets of lead to provide a waterproof covering.

Glass blowers produced hand-made glass for cathedral windows.

Stained-glass workers designed and made coloured glass windows.

Glass blower

Stained-glass craftsmen

J·E·J·MCMXCI

STONE TRACERY

Once the foundations for the cathedral were laid down, the architect and the master masons had to design and build the walls and windows. Walls, pillars and windows had a double function to perform. They had to be strong and sturdy enough to support the roof of the cathedral, but they also had to be beautiful to look at. The architect worked out his designs, probably sketching them on parchment, and perhaps copying some features from other buildings he had seen. Then he traced them out on the floor of a large covered space, where the masons could use them as life-size patterns to follow when carving their finished stonework.

For many of the most intricate sections of stonework, the masons first made wooden templates, or models, to guide them. These could be pieced together, trimmed and adjusted to ensure an exact fit. The most skilled workmen carried out all the elaborate and delicate stone carving, leaving the simpler sections of windows and arches to be completed by apprentices or less able workers.

Above right: Laying out designs for window tracery. Arches and carved pillars were copied from the architect's sketches by scratching the outlines into a thin layer of plaster spread on the tracing-room floor.

Wooden templates

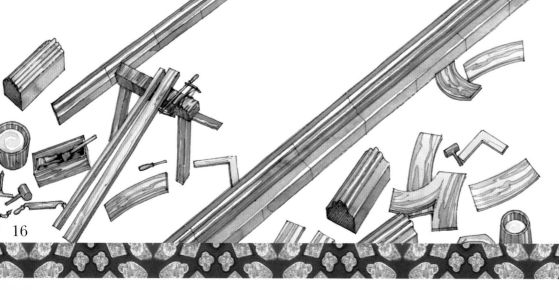

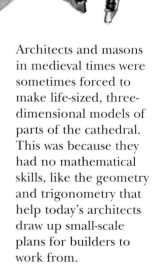

Architects and masons in medieval times were sometimes forced to make life-sized, three-dimensional models of parts of the cathedral. This was because they had no mathematical skills, like the geometry and trigonometry that help today's architects draw up small-scale plans for builders to work from.

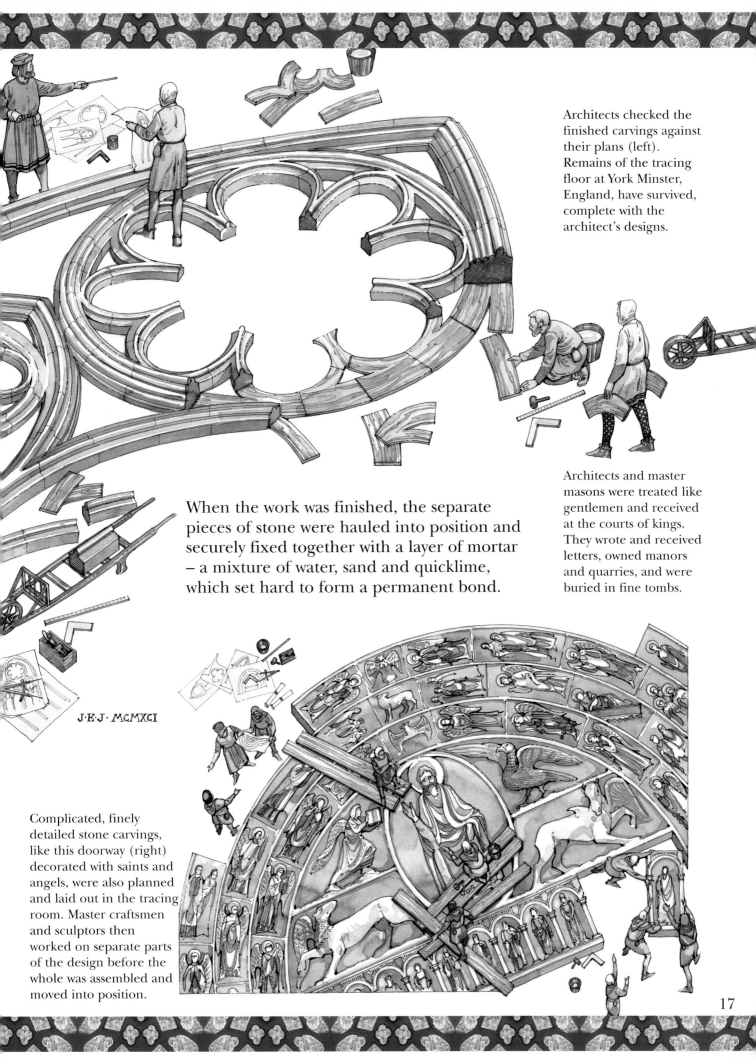

Architects checked the finished carvings against their plans (left). Remains of the tracing floor at York Minster, England, have survived, complete with the architect's designs.

When the work was finished, the separate pieces of stone were hauled into position and securely fixed together with a layer of mortar – a mixture of water, sand and quicklime, which set hard to form a permanent bond.

Architects and master masons were treated like gentlemen and received at the courts of kings. They wrote and received letters, owned manors and quarries, and were buried in fine tombs.

J·E·J· MCMXCI

Complicated, finely detailed stone carvings, like this doorway (right) decorated with saints and angels, were also planned and laid out in the tracing room. Master craftsmen and sculptors then worked on separate parts of the design before the whole was assembled and moved into position.

17

A WORKER'S DAY

Frame saw

Trestle

6 am (still dark) Gets up, washes hands and face, gets dressed.

6.30 am Breakfast with family: bread, cheese, skim milk, ale or cider.

7 am (sunrise) Off to work at the cathedral site in town.

7.30 am Takes orders from master carpenter; is sent to fetch wood.

9 am Returns from timber yard with piece of oak for carving.

10 am Dinner: meat pie, pancakes, ale, fetched from cooks' stalls.

10.30 am Back to work; starts to plane wood for door frame.

2 pm Called over to help move finished choir stalls into cathedral.

They have been carved in the lodges on site and are ready to be moved.

4 pm Stalls in place; carpenters thanked by man who paid for them.

6 pm (dusk) Time to go home; packs up tools and locks them in the lodge.

6.30 pm Back home for supper: dried pea soup, bread, ale. Hears gossip and news from family.

7.30 pm Commotion outside; a robbery from a house nearby. Cloth and pewter dishes taken.

All rush out to try to catch the thieves, but they escape and disappear down a dark alleyway.

9.30 pm A neighbour calls; reports that night watchman has caught the thieves red-handed.

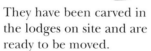

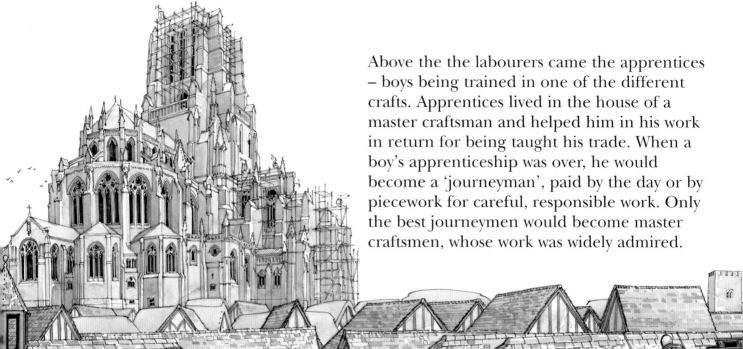

Above the the labourers came the apprentices – boys being trained in one of the different crafts. Apprentices lived in the house of a master craftsman and helped him in his work in return for being taught his trade. When a boy's apprenticeship was over, he would become a 'journeyman', paid by the day or by piecework for careful, responsible work. Only the best journeymen would become master craftsmen, whose work was widely admired.

Building a medieval cathedral might take hundreds of years, so whole colonies of workmen settled in the towns where cathedrals were being built. They knew there would always be work for them, and perhaps for their children and grandchildren, too. Medieval craftsmen worked from sunrise to sunset; this meant that their working day was longer in the summer. But they had many more holidays – to celebrate religious festivals, saints' days and traditional feasts – than most modern workers.

Not all craftsmen were hard-working. Often, the overseers on building sites complained about slackness and absenteeism. Many different kinds of workmen were involved in building a cathedral. At the lowest grade, there were untrained labourers, who did all the dirty, heavy jobs that required muscle power.

J·E·J· MCMXCI

The carpenter's wife is also busy all day. She cooks, cleans, shops, washes and mends clothes, and spins fine linen thread to sell.

BUILDING THE WALLS

Cathedral walls and pillars were massive structures, often enclosing an area hundreds of metres square. Although they were built of stone, they were not quite as solid as they looked. Usually, walls and pillars were constructed of two separate layers: an outer layer of neatly squared stone blocks, known as 'ashlar', carefully fitted together, and an inner core, or filling, of rough stone, rubble and mortar. Journeymen and labourers prepared the core, while skilled master masons chiselled the ashlar facing blocks. They often 'signed' these by carving their own 'mason's mark' into the finished piece of stone.

Designs and decorations used in cathedral building changed quite considerably over the centuries, although the basic plan of most cathedrals remained the same. The earliest surviving cathedrals, dating from the 10th to the 12th centuries, are built in a style known as 'Romanesque', with squat, solid pillars and heavy rounded arches. The elaborate doorway at the bottom of page 17 is in Romanesque style. Later medieval cathedrals dating from the 13th to the 15th centuries are built in a lighter style, usually known as Gothic. They have pointed arches, slender colums and soaring roofs, like the elegant section of Chartres Cathedral in France, shown here.

A 13th-century manuscript drawing shows masons and other craftsmen at work (opposite page, top left). The man on the left of the picture is using a level with an adjustable plumbline; below him, a man is hauling a basket of stones with a windlass. In the centre of the picture, a mason is checking the level of a newly positioned block of stone with a plumbline – there is a bowl of mortar by his feet – while below him, a skilled craftsman carves decorations for the top of a pillar. At the far right of the picture, a scaffolder perched halfway up a ladder bores a hole in a wooden post; below him, a carpenter shapes a beam with an axe.

Scaffolding was so important to the building work that it was often designed at the same time as the cathedral.

A scene portrayed in a 13th-century stained-glass window (far right) shows master masons at work. The man on the right of the picture is wearing a glove to protect his chisel-holding hand. The masons' templates (shapes used to help them cut complicated patterns) and compasses hang overhead. Their set squares (used to measure right angles) lie on the ground.

J·E·J·MCMXCI

Flying buttress

GUTTERS, GARGOYLES AND ROOFS

Once each section of the cathedral walls was completed, it had to be roofed over and made weatherproof. The earliest cathedral roofs were made of timber, but, whenever possible, these were replaced with stone, to lessen the risk of fire. But stone roofs were expensive, extremely heavy, and took a long time to build. Cathedral walls began to bulge outwards under the extra weight, and often had to be supported by rows of stone buttresses. Building these involved extra expense in materials and workmanship.

Nonetheless, the risk of fire – from stray sparks from nearby houses, from unattended candles, or occasionally from lightning – was so great that stone roofs were still preferred, despite the problems they brought. Medieval architects were also worried by the difficulties of carrying up the large quantities of water needed to put out fires. For this reason, they designed special stairs and passageways within the cathedral walls to allow firefighters quick and easy access to the roof.

Whatever they were made of, cathedral roofs still had to be covered with something to keep out the rain. Thin sheets of lead, which could be welded together to make a completely waterproof 'skin', were the first choice, but lead was expensive. Sometimes clay tiles or slates were used instead.

Gutters were essential to carry rainwater down from the high cathedral roof. Often, they were hidden in buttresses or pinnacles. Gargoyles were used as water spouts, to carry streams of rainwater away from the walls. Masons usually carved them like monsters or devils. But sometimes they made mocking portraits of bishops or craftsmen instead.

Long strips of lead, known as flashing, were used to cover gaps between roofs and walls. The edge of the flashing was curved back to stop water seeping in.

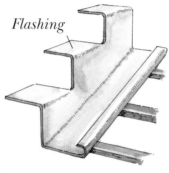

Flashing

Plumbers at work (opposite page, bottom right): First, sheets of lead were prepared from 'pigs' (solid blocks of lead). The pig was heated until it melted, and then the molten lead was poured into a level bed lined with sand. It was then left to cool. The finished sheets of lead were about one metre wide and several metres long. Though heavy, they were flexible and quite easy to work, and could be joined to form large sheets to cover a roof, or rolled around wooden posts to create drainpipes and gutters.

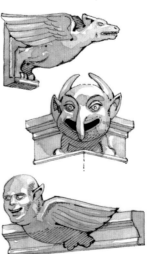

Gutter   *Pinnacle*

Gargoyles

The slope of a lead
roof could not be too
steep, or the heavy lead
might tear away and
roll down the roof like
a carpet.

J·E·J· MCMXLI

*Lead
casters*

Rolling lead sheets

FLOORS AND VAULTS

Even when the roof of a medieval cathedral was safely in place, the masons and stone carvers still had to decorate the ceiling, which worshippers could look up at and admire. The craftsmen also had to find a strong covering for the cathedral floor.

The earliest roofs were simple wooden rafters covered with slates or tiles. As building techniques developed, 'barrel vaults' were used. They were like the inside of a tunnel, with a row of semicircular arches supporting a smooth, curved surface in between. Roofs like this could be boarded over, or covered with plaster to form a plain ceiling. Later architects were more ambitious, and designed roofs with soaring, arched stone vaults. The stone arches formed a complicated pattern of criss-cross 'ribs' stretching diagonally across the space between the pillars. (The four drawings at the bottom of these pages show how this worked.) Over the years, ribs were arranged in ever more elaborate patterns. Eventually, most 'rib-vaulting' served no structural purpose at all, but was purely for decoration.

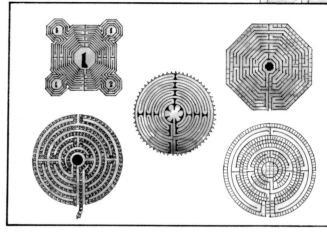

Above: Designs for mazes from five medieval cathedrals.

Below: Designs for windows, 11th to 14th centuries.

 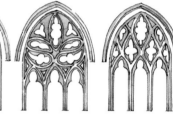

Cathedral floors were decorated with patterned tiles (below), made of

fired (baked) clay with designs in coloured and pigmented glazes.

Stages in building a rib-vaulted roof are shown here. First, a wooden framework (called 'centring') was made and put in position.

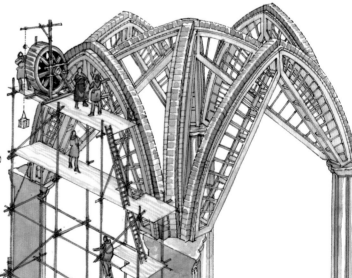

Then stone arches (or ribs) were built across the centring, criss-crossing the space above the pillars and forming a strong, lightweight 'cage'.

24

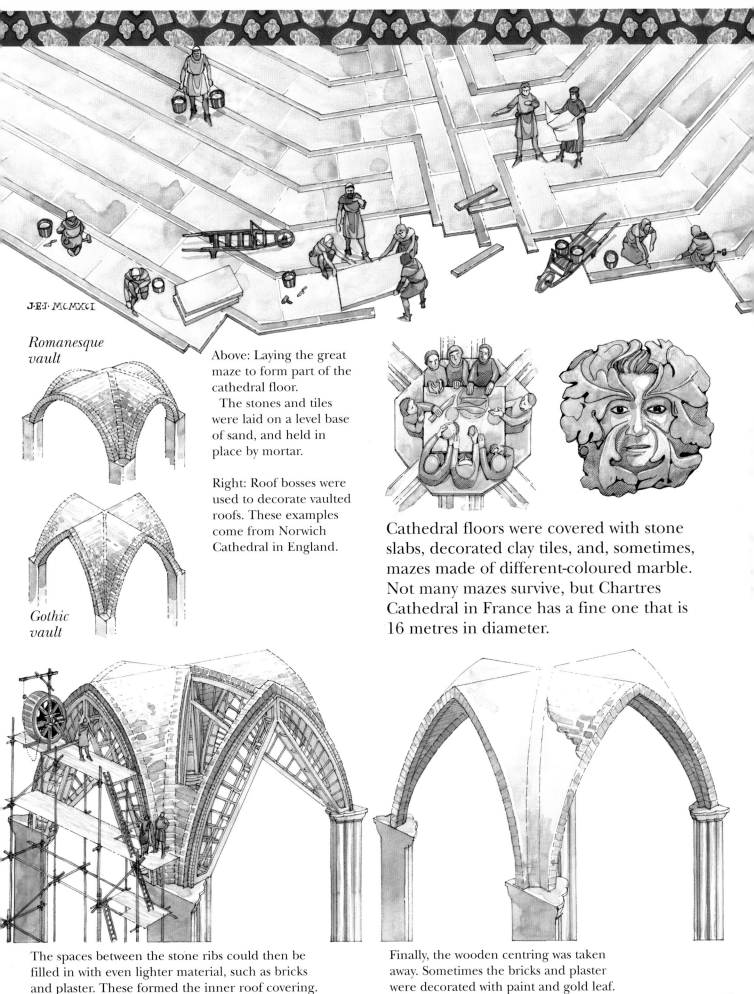

J·E·J· MCMXCI

Romanesque vault

Gothic vault

Above: Laying the great maze to form part of the cathedral floor.

The stones and tiles were laid on a level base of sand, and held in place by mortar.

Right: Roof bosses were used to decorate vaulted roofs. These examples come from Norwich Cathedral in England.

Cathedral floors were covered with stone slabs, decorated clay tiles, and, sometimes, mazes made of different-coloured marble. Not many mazes survive, but Chartres Cathedral in France has a fine one that is 16 metres in diameter.

The spaces between the stone ribs could then be filled in with even lighter material, such as bricks and plaster. These formed the inner roof covering.

Finally, the wooden centring was taken away. Sometimes the bricks and plaster were decorated with paint and gold leaf.

'THE BIBLE OF THE POOR'

Towards the end of the 15th century, the French poet François Villon wrote the following lines describing how his mother, a poor peasant woman, might feel when she walked into her beautifully decorated local village church:

I am a woman, poor and old,
Quite ignorant, I cannot read.
They showed me, in my village church,
A painted Paradise with harps,
And Hell where the damned souls are boiled.
One gives me joy, the other frightens me...

Until the later Middle Ages, most ordinary people could not read or understand the words of church services, which were in Latin. The only ways they had of learning about Christianity were by listening to sermons or by looking at the scenes from saints' lives and Bible stories shown in wall paintings, statues and stained glass.

The brilliantly coloured glass used in medieval cathedrals was made in special workshops established in major towns. Chemicals were mixed with the molten glass to produce glowing colours, and the designs were pieced together and held secure by thin strips of lead. In the 14th century, craftsmen discovered a way of painting on glass using a special silver stain, to add greater richness and detail to their designs.

Installing a great 'rose window'. These dramatic circular windows were first introduced during the 12th century in France, and became very popular. The circular designs were thought to represent the petals of a flower opening towards the sun. Rose windows gave craftsmen a chance to show their skill, and still survive at Chartres Cathedral in France, and York Minster in England.

Stained glass windows took skilled craftsmen many hours to build. First, glass was made by melting sand, lime and potash together. The glass blower then blew the molten glass into a cylindrical shape, which was cut open and flattened. The glass worker cut the glass roughly according to the window design by touching it with a hot iron and pouring cold water over the heated areas, causing the glass to break along the 'hot spots'. Workers then used a tool called a 'grozing iron' to cut the glass into smaller pieces. The glass was then painted with a special paint which, when heated, melted into the glass. The glass pieces were fitted together with lengths of lead called 'cames', and the joints fixed with drops of molten solder, a mixture of lead and tin.

BELL TOWERS AND SPIRES

Cathedrals were built to be noticed. First of all, they were designed to give honour and glory to God, but they also brought fame and a measure of fortune to the men who designed and built them, and to the towns where they stood. One of the best ways of making a huge cathedral even more noticeable was by adding to its height by building a tower or a spire. These tall 'fingers' also pointed to heaven, and so served as a constant reminder of God to all.

Towers also had a useful purpose, for housing clocks and bells. Peals of bells were rung to summon worshippers to services in churches and cathedrals. In the early Middle Ages clocks were unknown, so time was measured by specially marked candles (which burned a known length per hour), or, more usually, by hourglasses filled with sand, and sundials fixed on outside walls. But by the 13th century, medieval scientists and engineers began to design mechanical devices to tell the time. The earliest surviving European clock, as we would recognise it today, is thought to be the one in Salisbury Cathedral, England. Bells and clocks were given to cathedrals in the hope of winning God's pardon for sins, or in memory of well-loved or famous people who had died.

Bishops and townspeople competed to build the largest and most beautiful cathedral. The tallest medieval spire was at Strasbourg in France. Almost 150 m high (as high as a 45-storey building today), it remained the tallest building in Europe for hundreds of years, until the Eiffel Tower was built in Paris during the 19th century using newly invented cast iron.

Bells were cast in moulds (right). First, a full-size model of the bell was made from clay (1). It was coated with a layer of wax (2) and covered with more clay, leaving a few channels leading to the outside (3). The whole block was heated, and the liquid wax trickled away (4). Melted bell-metal was then poured into the mould to replace the wax (5). It was left to harden, and then the clay mould was broken open. The bell then had to be smoothed and finished by hand (6).

The spire on the opposite page is made of stone. But most spires were made of wood, covered with thin sheets of lead, which made them very heavy. They were fragile and liable to be blown down in high winds.

Because they were covered with metal, spires were often struck by lightning. Many cathedrals were damaged when their tall spires and heavy bell towers crashed to the ground, smashing through the roof and damaging the nave.

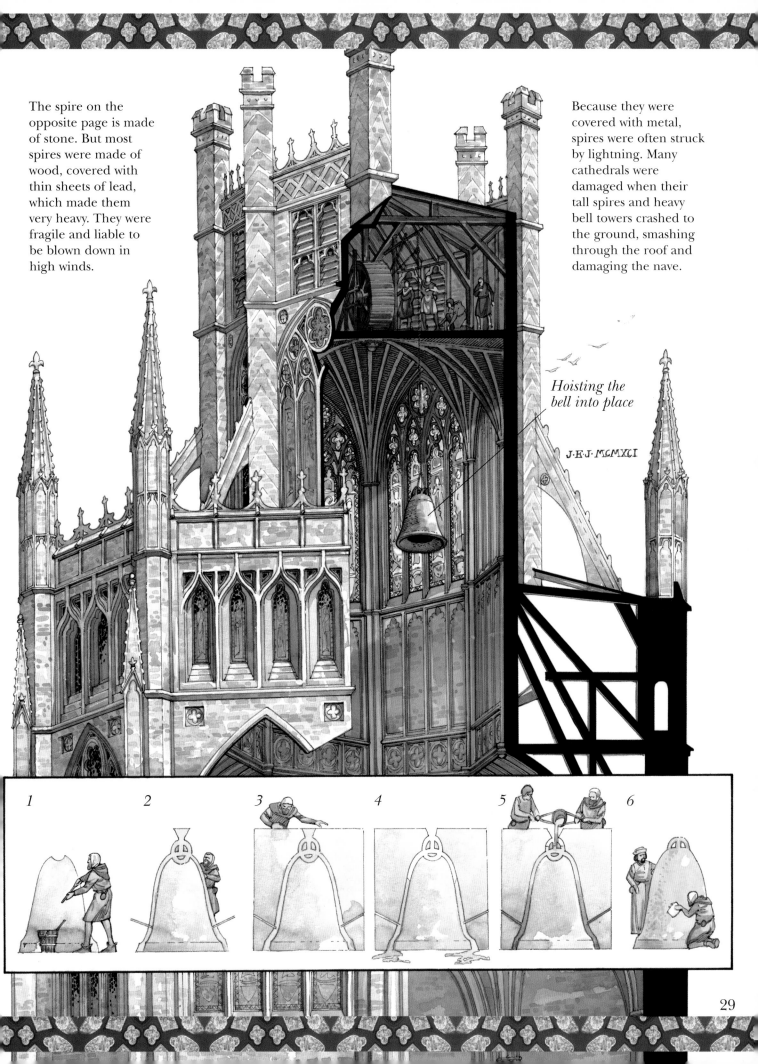

Hoisting the bell into place

J·E·J·MCMXCI

1

2

3

4

5

6

VISIONS OF HEAVEN

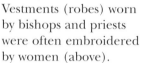

Medieval churches and cathedrals were decorated with wall paintings, carvings, statues and other precious objects to add to their beauty and splendour. However, as Abbot Suger, head of the French abbey of St Denis, wrote in the early 12th century, displaying these treasures had another purpose: to 'show simple people…what they must believe'. Churches and cathedrals, glittering with gold and jewels, glowing with light and colour, and headily perfumed with incense, must often have seemed to 'simple people' like a foretaste of Heaven, at least as medieval preachers described it.

Among the most sumptuous of medieval cathedral treasures were richly embroidered robes, altar cloths, banners and wall hangings. Craftworkers, monks and nuns produced many outstanding embroideries. English church embroidery was especially famous. When the Normans invaded England in 1066, one of William the Conqueror's barons reported that 'The women of England are very skilful with the needle.' He praised the elaborate cloths worked with silk and gold that were exported throughout Europe. When Thomas Selmiston, an English monk, died in 1419, he was mourned because 'He was in the art of embroidery a most cunning artificer (craftsman), having none like him.'

Above left: Split stitch, one of the most commonly used stitches in medieval embroidery.

Vestments (robes) worn by bishops and priests were often embroidered by women (above).

Tapestries and embroidered hangings were stretched on a frame (above) to support the weight of the fabric while it was worked.

Artists made their own paints (above and right), using pestles and mortars for mixing and grinding. Colour came from powdered pigments – minerals such as lapis lazuli (a beautiful and very expensive blue) or red lead. To make paint, the pigment was mixed with a sticky, liquid medium which sometimes contained egg yolks or 'size' made from boiled animal hoofs and horns.

Thin sheets of pure gold, known as gold leaf, were also glued to paintings to add richness and lustre.

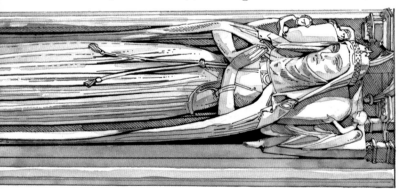

Above: Alabaster tomb effigy (life-size statue) of Alice de la Pole, duchess of Suffolk, who died in 1475.

Right: Elaborately decorated tomb, carved around 1330, of Marie de Valois, Queen of Naples in Italy.

J·E·J·MCMXCI

Priests and people

Since cathedrals were so large, and took so long to build, many of the bishops must have spent the whole of their period in office attempting to hold services or run their dioceses in the middle of a vast building site. What were a medieval bishop's responsibilities towards the people – and buildings – in his care?

One writer of the Middle Ages described the duties of a bishop like this: 'His prayers first, then his book-work, reading or writing, teaching or learning; and then his church hours (services) at the right time;…and his almsgiving;…and the supervision of work… and, at public meetings, he ought often and frequently to teach knowledge of the Christian faith among the people…' Throughout the Middle Ages, bishops' spiritual duties remained much the same, and they are very similar today.

Many bishops also played an active part in politics, acting as government ministers and advisors to kings and princes. In medieval England, bishops were summoned to Parliament, where they sat in the House of Lords. Bishops were also responsible for all the priests, monks and nuns in their dioceses, and for administering the large estates that had been given by wealthy and religious people to help build and maintain their cathedrals.

1. A candlestick of enormous proportions, from the abbey of St Remi at Reims, France.
2. A box made of gold and jewels, containing the relics of a saint.
3. A gold container shaped like a dove.
4. A gilt and bronze lectern (reading stand).

5. Ivory carving showing Jesus on the cross.
6. Top part of a bishop's crozier (staff), made of gold and silver.
7. A model rose, made of gold, silver and jewels, from Basle, Switzerland.
8. A cross carried in processions, made of silver and decorated with exquisite enamel-work.
9. A female artist painting a self-portrait.

The bishop wore magnificent robes while taking services or preaching sermons. This was originally done out of respect for God, but some bishops also basked in the glory of their own, and their cathedral's, power.

Priest

Bishop

Pope

The bishop also wore a pointed hat, known as a mitre, and carried a tall staff called a crozier. This was based on a shepherd's crook, and was meant to remind the bishop to care for ordinary people as a shepherd cares for his flock. The bishop's robe, mitre and crook were often made out of rich, costly materials, and ornamented with gold, silver and jewels.

PILGRIMS

Men and women from all over medieval Europe travelled long distances on pilgrimage, to visit the tombs where saints or other holy people had been buried. Some pilgrims ventured further afield to the 'Holy Land' (the area around Jerusalem) where Jesus lived and died. Christians believed that time spent on religious journeys such as these would help win forgiveness for their sins and perhaps earn them a place in Heaven. Pilgrimages also provided the opportunity for an enjoyable, although sometimes rather dangerous, holiday in pleasant company. Special pilgrimage routes became established, with shops and hostels along the way. Bandits and highway robbers also seized rich pickings from pilgrims by ambushing them in wild and lonely country.

A French writer of the 12th century described a group of pilgrims setting out: 'The day was clear and calm. The girls and young men all recited poems or songs, and even the old people began to sing again. They all seemed joyful…Even the little birds sang happily… On the hillside…the cooks have set up tents…There were many different wines, breads and pies, fruit and fish, birds, cakes and venison…plenty to buy for anyone who had money.'

Canterbury

Winchester

Chartres

Reims

Cologne

Sainte Chapelle, Paris

Notre Dame, Paris

Santiago de Compostela

Toulouse

Pilgrim

Scrip

Pilgrims' badges

Staff

J·E·J· MCMXCI

St Mark's, Venice

Old St Peter's, Rome

····▶ *To Jerusalem*

Pilgrims dressed sensibly for their travels. They carried clothing, food, money and a prayer book in a leather satchel known as a 'scrip'. Pilgrims travelling on foot carried long sticks to support them on the rocky paths. They sometimes bought little badges, made of metal or cloth, in the towns near the saints' shrines. They sewed these onto their cloaks to prove they had really been on pilgrimage. One of the most popular places of pilgrimage was the Cathedral of St James (or Santiago) at Compostela in Spain. Its badge was a scallop shell.

On their journeys, pilgrims stayed at inns or hostels like this one from a 14th-century drawing.

Some priests and preachers criticised pilgrims for enjoying themselves too much.

Medieval reliquaries

Cathedrals that housed the relics (remains) of popular saints could be sure of attracting many pilgrims. Beautiful, jewelled display cases, called reliquaries, were built to house saints' bones or other holy objects.

Pilgrims offered money to see these, and paid extra to touch or kiss them. They hoped the saint's prayers would help them, and maybe even bring about a miraculous cure from some deadly disease.

35

MIRACLE PLAYS

Miracle or 'mystery' plays were a form of entertainment often associated with cathedrals. They consisted of scenes from the Bible, acted out at appropriate seasons of the Church's year, with dressing up, singing and dancing. These plays originated as part of special festival services, with monks or priests performing all the parts. In Winchester cathedral in England, monks sang Easter choruses like this around 970:

Alleluia, the Lord is risen today,
The strong lion is risen, Christ, the son of God.
Thanks be to God, raise the joyful cry.

Later in the Middle Ages, ordinary people took part in these plays, which were performed outside cathedrals. Some church leaders disapproved. As the priest William of Wadington wrote around 1300 in a book called *The Manual of Sins*: 'Foolish clerks have devised another clear folly, which they call "miracles". Their faces are disguised by masks…they make foolish assemblies in city streets or in graveyards after meals, when fools are glad to come. Even though they say it is done for a good purpose, do not on any account believe them that it is done for the honour of God, but rather in truth for that of the devil.'

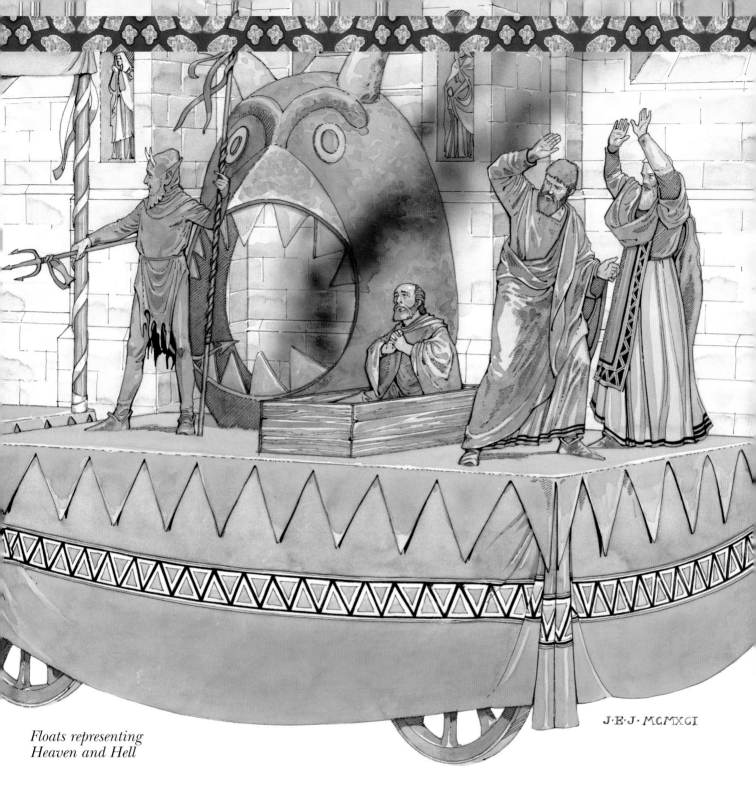

*Floats representing
Heaven and Hell*

Some of the props and costumes used in the miracle plays performed in 1565 are described below: 'A Griffon (a dragon-like monster); a rib bone, coloured red; 2 coats and 2 pairs of dyed hose (tights) for Eve; a dyed coat and hose for Adam; a mask and wig for God the Father; 2 wigs for Adam and Eve.'

Although actors often worked for free, they sometimes received good wages for taking part in the miracle plays, as this record of payment made in Yorkshire, England, in 1483 shows: 'To the minstrels, 6d.; To Noah and his wife, 1s. 6d.; To Robert Brown playing God, 6d.'

Throughout Europe, church festivals were often celebrated by processions. The Procession of the Holy Blood was a Belgian celebration, while in Spain worshippers celebrated the feast of Corpus Christi. The French held processions for the festival of Saintes Maries de la Mer.

Cathedral clergy carried tall crosses, candles and banners – often acting out events in the life of Jesus as they went – while the choir followed, singing hymns. Ordinary people either joined in the procession, or knelt by the roadside, waiting for the bishop to bless them as he passed.

Monasteries

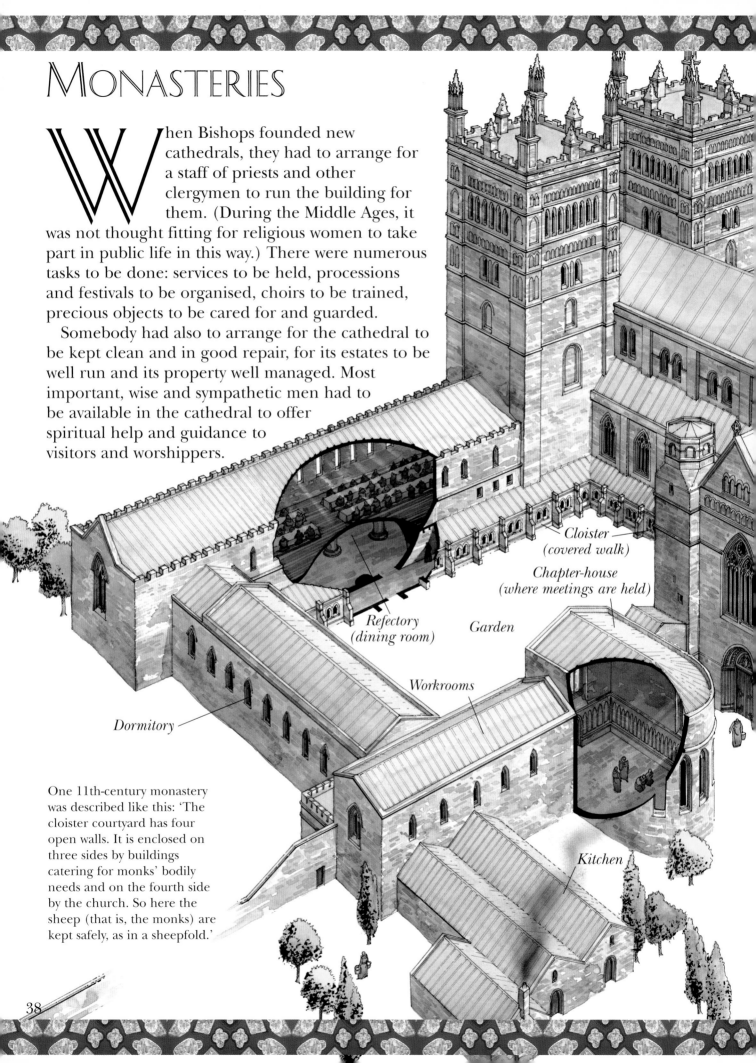

When Bishops founded new cathedrals, they had to arrange for a staff of priests and other clergymen to run the building for them. (During the Middle Ages, it was not thought fitting for religious women to take part in public life in this way.) There were numerous tasks to be done: services to be held, processions and festivals to be organised, choirs to be trained, precious objects to be cared for and guarded.

Somebody had also to arrange for the cathedral to be kept clean and in good repair, for its estates to be well run and its property well managed. Most important, wise and sympathetic men had to be available in the cathedral to offer spiritual help and guidance to visitors and worshippers.

One 11th-century monastery was described like this: 'The cloister courtyard has four open walls. It is enclosed on three sides by buildings catering for monks' bodily needs and on the fourth side by the church. So here the sheep (that is, the monks) are kept safely, as in a sheepfold.'

Cloister
(covered walk)

Chapter-house
(where meetings are held)

Refectory
(dining room)

Garden

Workrooms

Dormitory

Kitchen

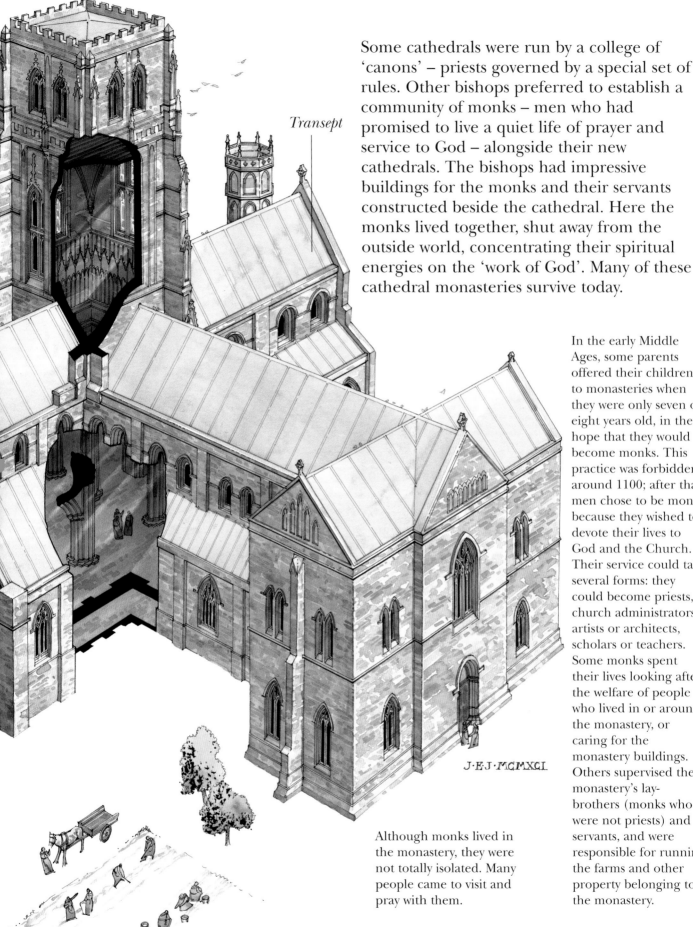

Transept

Some cathedrals were run by a college of 'canons' – priests governed by a special set of rules. Other bishops preferred to establish a community of monks – men who had promised to live a quiet life of prayer and service to God – alongside their new cathedrals. The bishops had impressive buildings for the monks and their servants constructed beside the cathedral. Here the monks lived together, shut away from the outside world, concentrating their spiritual energies on the 'work of God'. Many of these cathedral monasteries survive today.

In the early Middle Ages, some parents offered their children to monasteries when they were only seven or eight years old, in the hope that they would become monks. This practice was forbidden around 1100; after that, men chose to be monks because they wished to devote their lives to God and the Church. Their service could take several forms: they could become priests, church administrators, artists or architects, scholars or teachers. Some monks spent their lives looking after the welfare of people who lived in or around the monastery, or caring for the monastery buildings. Others supervised the monastery's lay-brothers (monks who were not priests) and servants, and were responsible for running the farms and other property belonging to the monastery.

J·E·J·MCMXCI

Although monks lived in the monastery, they were not totally isolated. Many people came to visit and pray with them.

A DAY IN THE LIFE OF A MONK

1 am – 2 am In church for first services.

3 am Back to bed for a few more hours' sleep.

6 am get up and wash. Prayers in church.

10 am Main meal: fish, bread, eggs, vegetables.

7 am Breakfast: bread, cheese, ale or cider.

7.30 am – 9 am At work in the monastery garden.

9 am Back in church for more prayers.

10.30 am – 12 noon Clean buildings.

12 noon In church for midday services.

1 pm – 6 pm More work, writing or studying.

6 pm In church for evening service.

6.30 pm Supper (soup), followed by quiet rest and relaxation. Guests often

came to talk to the monks, or just to drink and play music.

8.00 pm Back in church for the final service of the day.

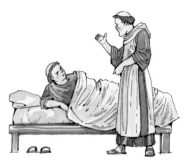

8.30 pm Bed in dormitory shared with the other monks.

During the Middle Ages, many bishops began their careers as scholars. They often invited other men of learning to visit their cathedrals to study or to preach. And many cathedrals supported a community of scholars in a monastery close by. According to the rule of St Benedict, which governed the lives of thousands of monks living in these cathedral monasteries, the monks' time should be divided between useful work and prayer. Often this 'work' meant studying, writing or teaching.

Some cathedral monasteries became great centres of book production, where monks copied out and illuminated (decorated with paintings) beautiful Bibles and psalters used in cathedral services or for private prayers. Other monasteries were well known for their collections of important books on religious an learned topics. For example, Hereford Cathedral in England still has its magnificent medieval chained library. The books are fastened to the walls with heavy iron chains, to stop them being taken away by thieves or absent-minded scholars. Precautions like these were necessary, since all medieval books were valuable. Because they were written and bound entirely by hand, only a few copies were produced. A single volume could easily take hundreds of hours of hard work.

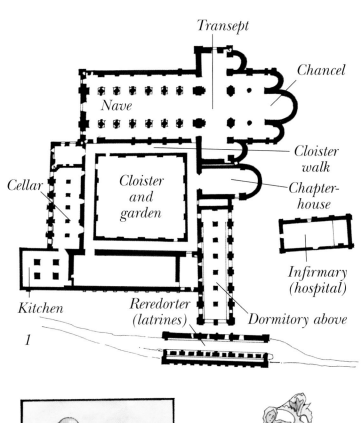

1

2

3

J·E·J· MCMXCI

1. Plan of a typical medieval monastery.
2. A monk painting, from a manuscript. Some monks and nuns were great illustrators.
3. An elaborate manuscript illustration.
4. Wealthy parents sent their children to be educated by monks and nuns: boys went to monasteries, girls to nunneries. The monks taught children how to read and write in Latin.

4

Past and Present

Although we usually think of the Middle Ages as the great age of cathedral building, bishops and their congregations have continued to plan and raise funds for the construction of magnificent cathedrals right up to the present day. Older cathedrals have also been completed, enlarged or sometimes – like York Minster and Coventry Cathedral, both in England – carefully rebuilt after damage in war or as a result of natural disasters.

Why do people continue to build cathedrals? What makes men and women today devote their lives to such enormous and time-consuming projects? Usually, their reasons are similar to those of the medieval bishops and their patrons: they are building to give glory to God and to draw attention to the Church's Christian message. No doubt they also welcome the opportunity to spend their lives creating something well made, strong and beautiful.

Liverpool Roman Catholic Cathedral in England. It was built between 1960 and 1966, using modern materials such as concrete and steel.

Reims Cathedral in France. Building stopped in 1427, halfway up the cathedral's towers.

St Basil's Cathedral in Moscow, Russia, built in typical Russian style between 1555 and 1560.

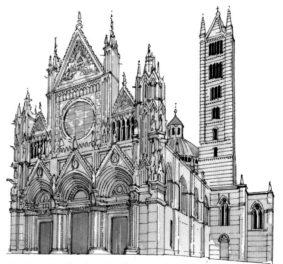

Church of the Holy Family in Barcelona, Spain, begun in 1882 and not yet finished.

Cologne Cathedral in Germany, a medieval cathedral with one spire added in the 19th century.

Milan Cathedral in Italy, a striking white marble building designed by a French architect and begun in 1386, but not finished until 1809, under the orders of the French emperor Napoleon.

Above: Gargoyle portraying a workman, on Washington DC Cathedral, USA.

Left: The 'Space Window' in Washington DC Cathedral.

Washington DC Cathedral, USA. Built during the 20th century in a medieval Gothic style using traditional building techniques.

But most of all, at a time when the future looks uncertain and nothing seems built to last, modern cathedral builders are making a statement of faith. Like the architects and craftsmen who worked on the medieval cathedrals, they are building not just for the present, but for the years to come, and, perhaps, even for eternity.

Below: The Cathedral of St John the Divine in New York, USA. Work began in 1892, and the cathedral is still unfinished. Instead, money is spent to help poor and needy people in the diocese.

The bell tower of St Mark's Cathedral in Venice stood for exactly a thousand years. The foundations were laid in 902, and the tower collapsed suddenly in 1902.

Cathedrals staffed by monks were famous for their charitable giving during the Middle Ages. For example, at Norwich Cathedral in England the almoner – a monk with special responsibility for helping poor and sick people – gave out more than 10,000 loaves of bread each year. The monastic kitchens at Norwich also used 10,000 eggs a week. Even though medieval eggs are supposed to have been much smaller than today's eggs, it is still a surprisingly large number of eggs to get through each week!

In 1239, the tower at Lincoln Cathedral in England crashed down during a service. Three people were killed and many others were injured. So it is not surprising that one prayer said at lincoln cathedral contained the words: 'Deare Lord, support our roof this night, that it may in no wise fall upon us and styfle (suffocate) us, Amen.'

Enormous quantities of material were used to build the great medieval cathedrals. For example, just one tower – the 'lantern' of Ely Cathedral in England – contains over 400 tons of wood and lead.

Cathedrals are very expensive to build. To help raise funds for building St Peter's in Rome in 1507, Pope Urban proclaimed an indulgence – pardon for all their sins – to people who gave money to the cathedral building funds.

The 13th century was a great age of cathedral building: 1220 saw building work begin on no fewer than three cathedrals: Amiens in France, Salisbury in England, and Brussels in Belgium.

The Dome of the Rock in Jerusalem is the only building in the world to have been sacred to three religions. It was founded as a Jewish temple, became a Christian cathedral, and is now a Muslim mosque.

There has been a church on the site of Cologne Cathedral in Germany ever since 873. The present cathedral dates from 1248. Its spire, however, was only added to the cathedral in the 19th century. The workmen followed designs that had been drawn up by medieval architects and had survived, unharmed, for almost 400 years.

The Cathedral of Santa Maria del Fiore in Florence, Italy, was probably the fastest cathedral ever to be built, completed in only 14 years between 1420 and 1433. While the great dome was being built, its architect Filippo Brunelleschi even had temporary restaurants and wine shops built up in the dome so that the masons would not have to make the tiring journey down and up again at lunchtime.

The first Russian cathedral was founded in 1050; it is the Cathedral of Santa Sofia in Novgorod.

In Anglo-Saxon times, a monastic chronicler recorded a rather grisly list of relics that had been preserved in Canterbury Cathedral in England because of their holiness and supposed power. It began with the altar that was used every day for services, where 'the blessed (Bishop) Elphege had solemnly deposited the head of St Swithin…and also many relics of other saints.' The list ended with the head 'of the blessed virgin Austroberta.'

St Paul's Cathedral in London burned down and was rebuilt twice. The first fire was in 1087, the second in 1666.

A simple early cathedral

Old St Peter's, Rome

St Mark's, Venice

Santiago de Compostela

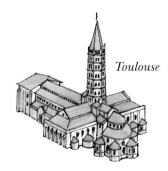

Toulouse

Styles of cathedral building have changed over the centuries, from small, simple buildings to grand, towering constructions. On this page you can see some examples of cathedral architecture, and note how the shape, size and design of medieval cathedrals developed through the years.

The earliest cathedrals were simple structures, built out of local materials, either wood or stone. Often, a rounded apse was added to a small, rectangular church to house the *cathedra*, or bishop's throne. Before long, wealthy bishops extended and expanded this arrangement, adding towers, porches and extra buildings, as you can see in the drawing of Old St Peter's in Rome, Italy. Building started here during the 4th century and the cathedral was added to several times during the centuries that followed.

Other early cathedrals were influenced by local styles of architecture. For example, St Mark's in Venice, Italy, was built during the 9th century in a Byzantine style, copied from cathedrals and churches the architect had seen in eastern Mediterranean countries.

Romanesque cathedrals, like Santiago de Compostela in Spain, and Toulouse in the south of France (both built during the 11th

Chartres

Notre Dame, Paris

Reims

Canterbury

Cologne

century), also developed the simple basic plan of early cathedrals, using massive pillars and heavy, rounded arches to give strength and solidity to their construction. At Santiago, tall towers were built at the west end to create an impressive entrance.

By the late 12th and early 13th centuries, cathedral architects began to experiment with new styles and techniques of cathedral building. In the earliest Gothic cathedrals, for example, of Chartres and Notre Dame, Paris (both in France), the rounded arches and heavy pillars of the Romanesque style of architecture were replaced by taller, slender columns and pointed arches. Windows were larger, allowing space for brilliant stained glass, and roofs were higher.

This graceful new Gothic style was developed further in the 13th-century cathedrals, such as Reims in France, which are remarkable for their light and elegant design. By the 14th and 15th centuries, Gothic architecture became amazingly complicated, daring and elaborate, as you can see in the beautiful stonework decorating the famous late-medieval cathedrals at Canterbury in England, and at Cologne in Germany.

GLOSSARY

Aisle An extension built on either side of a church's nave and running its whole length. ('Aisle' comes from the old French word for 'wing'.)

Almoner A monk whose duties included giving money and food to poor and needy people.

Alms-giving Giving money to charity.

Altar A table, usually made of stone and covered with richly decorated cloth, where the Church service, known as Mass, was celebrated by bishops and priests. Cathedrals might have several altars, some in separate chapels dedicated to saints. The most important altar was called the high altar, and the most holy area of the cathedral was the space around the high altar.

Apse A semicircular area at the east end of a church or a cathedral, usually behind the high altar.

Arcade A row of arches supported by pillars.

Ashlar Stone that has been carefully cut and shaped into neat, even blocks.

Buttress A prop or support made of stone, designed to stop cathedral walls collapsing outwards under the weight of the roof.

Byzantine A word used to describe people, objects or designs for art and architecture originating in the Byzantine Empire. In the Middle Ages, this powerful state ruled over an area including present-day Greece and Turkey, and the neighbouring lands.

Cathedra A Greek word meaning 'throne'. Cathedrals took their name from the fact that each of them contained a bishop's cathedra, or throne.

Choir The area of the cathedral closest to the high altar. Cathedral clergy, including the bishop, stood in the choir during religious services.

Diocese The area cared for and administered by a bishop.

Flying buttress A narrow, graceful buttress shaped like half an arch.

Foundation A solid platform below ground, built to support the weight of a cathedral or any other building.

Galilee A large, decorated porch built onto the west end of a cathedral. It was named after an area in the Holy Land where Jesus preached.

Gargoyles Spouts and gutters used to direct rain away from the cathedral walls. Gargoyles were often carved to represent monsters or people with strange or funny faces.

Holy Land The area around the city of Jerusalem (which is in present-day Israel). Christians believe it is holy because Jesus lived and died there.

Indulgence Forgiveness of sins granted by the Church, in return for a payment of money. Usually the money was given to a good cause, such as helping the poor or paying for a new cathedral building.

Journeyman A fully trained craftsmen who worked and was paid by the day.

Mortar A mixture of sand, quicklime and water, used to 'sandwich' blocks of building stone together. Mortar sets hard as it dries, but crumbles over the years and sometimes needs replacing.

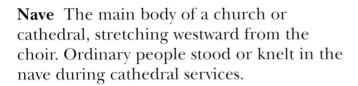

Nave The main body of a church or cathedral, stretching westward from the choir. Ordinary people stood or knelt in the nave during cathedral services.

Oratory A place where people say prayers.

Parchment Specially treated skins of sheep or goats, used to write on during the Middle Ages before paper became widely available.

Pigment A coloured powder, made of earth, stone or chemical salts, mixed with size or glue to make paint.

Pillar A tall, straight column of wood, or more usually of stone, used to support the roof of a building.

Porch A small building covering a doorway, and providing shelter for clergy and worshippers entering or leaving the cathedral.

Psalter A book of psalms. Psalms are songs and poems in praise of God composed thousands of years ago by David, king of the Jews. They form part of the Bible, and can be found in the Old Testament.

Quicklime A compound of the mineral calcium used in making mortar. It gives off heat when mixed with water, and rapidly sets hard.

Relics The holy remains – often including bones, hair or clothes – of saints. Other relics revered by medieval cathedral visitors included fragments of the cross on which Jesus was crucified, and thorns from the crown of thorns he wore on the cross. Relics were not worshipped themselves, but were used to help people remember the Christian message and be inspired by the lives of the Christian saints.

Reliquary A container for relics, often made of gold and silver and decorated with precious stones.

Rib-vaulting Delicate stonework used to decorate the underside of a roof vault.

Roof boss A cluster of carved stonework, usually circular in shape, used to decorate the points where the criss-cross ribs used on roof vaults meet. Many roof bosses are beautifully decorated with carvings showing scenes from Bible stories, or bunches of leaves and flowers. Some portray magical and mysterious creatures as well.

Rose window A large circular window filled with brilliantly coloured glass.

Spire A tall, pointed structure built on top of a cathedral tower, often topped by a weather vane or a cross.

Template A pattern showing the shape of an object that needs to be made.

Tie beam A thick, strong wooden beam forming part of a roof. They are called tie beams because they stretch across the roof space and hold together the timber framework of the roof.

Tracery A pattern of interlacing lines.

Transept A sideways extension of a cathedral (or any church), usually built at the point where the nave joins the choir. The ground plans of churches and cathedrals with transepts are cross-shaped.

Vault The arched underside of the roof. It could be covered with stone tracery (see 'rib-vaulting', above), wooden planks or plaster. Often, cathedral roofs were decorated with paintings, carvings, or gold and silver leaf.

INDEX Page numbers in bold refer to illustrations.